THE COLD WAR CHRONICLES

Superpower Rivalries and Proxy Warfare

Avery Elizabeth Hurt

Cavendish Square
New York

Published in 2018 by Cavendish Square Publishing, LLC
243 5th Avenue, Suite 136, New York, NY 10016

First Edition

Website: cavendishsq.com

CPSIA Compliance Information: Batch #CS17CSQ

All websites were available and accurate when this book was sent to press.

Library of Congress Cataloging-in-Publication Data

Names: Hurt, Avery Elizabeth.
Title: Superpower rivalries and proxy warfare / Avery Elizabeth Hurt.
Description: New York : Cavendish Square, 2018. | Series: The Cold War chronicles | Includes index.
Identifiers: ISBN 9781502627292 (library bound) | ISBN 9781502627254 (ebook)
Subjects: LCSH: Cold War--Juvenile literature. | World politics--1945-1989--Juvenile literature.
Classification: LCC D843.H87 2018 | DDC 909.82--dc23

Editorial Director: David McNamara
Editor: Jodyanne Benson
Copy Editor: Rebecca Rohan
Associate Art Director: Amy Greenan
Designer: Alan Sliwinski
Production Coordinator: Karol Szymczuk
Photo Research: J8 Media

The photographs in this book are used by permission and through the courtesy of: Cover mary delaney cooke/Corbis via Getty Images; p. 4 Radharc Images/Alamy Stock Photo; p. 8 Sovfoto/UIG via Getty Images; p. 10 Lockeyear W T (Capt), Malindine E G (Capt), No 5 Army Film & Photographic Unit/Wikimedia Commons/File:Britain's new Prime Minister, Clement Attlee, with President Truman and Marshal Stalin at the Potsdam Conference in Berlin, 1 August 1945. BU9496.jpg; p. 12 Roger Viollet Collection/Getty Images; p. 17 Abbie Rowe/ Wikimedia Commons/File:Photograph of President Truman waving his hat and Winston; p. Churchill flashing his famous "V for Victory" sign from the... - NARA -199350.jpg/CC-SA; p. 19 Abbie Rowe/Wikimedia Commons/File:Photograph of President Truman at his desk in the Oval Office, signing the National Security Act Amendments of 1949... - NARA -200168.jpg/CC-SA; p. 22 Sovfoto/UIG via Getty Images; p. 24-25 United States Department of Defense/Wikimedia Commons/File:Operation Crossroads Baker Edit.jpg; p. 28 Art Media/ Print Collector/Getty Images; p. 32 Bettmann/Getty Images; p. 34 Bettmann/Getty Images; p. 37 Brandon Bourdages/Shutterstock.com; p. 43 Everett Historical/Shutterstock.com; p. 45 Nikita Khrushchev/Wikimedia Commons/File:Khrushchev letter to kennedy.gif/CC-SA; p. 47 TASS via Getty Images; p. 50 U.S. National Archives and Records Administration/Wikimedia Commons/File:Soviet Prime Minister Josef Stalin poses with President Harry S. Truman during the Potsdam Conference in Germany. V.... -NARA - 198836.jpg/CC-SA; p. 52 U.S. Army Signal Corps officer Gaetano Faillace/Wikimedia Commons/File:Douglas MacArthur lands Leyte1.jpg/CC-SA; p. 58 Warren K. Leffler/ Wikimedia Commons/File:Nikita Khrushchev 1960.jpg/CC-SA; p. 63 © Hulton-Deutsch Collection/CORBIS/Corbis via Getty Images; p. 65 © Wally McNamee/CORBIS/Corbis via Getty Images; p. 68-69 Howard Ruffner/Getty Images; p. 72 Ron Case/Getty Images; p. 75 The Central Intelligence Agency/Wikimedia Commons/File:Nixon and Kissinger - Flickr - The Central Intelligence Agency.jpg; p. 76 Byron E. Schumaker/Wikimedia Commons/File:President and Mrs. Nixon visit the Great Wall of China.jpg; p. 81 USAF/Wikimedia Commons/ File:Boeing B-52 dropping bombs.jpg; p. 82 Peter Hamer/Wikimedia Commons/File:Ken Thompson (sitting) and Dennis Ritchie at PDP-11; p. (2876612463).jpg; p. 86 Alain Nogues/Sygma/Sygma via Getty Images; p. 90-91 Thomas Imo/Photothek via Getty Images; p. 95 TASS via Getty Images; p. 97 Sergei Guneyev/The LIFE Images Collection/Getty Images; p. 99 NICHOLAS KAMM/AFP/Getty Images.

Printed in the United States of America

CONTENTS

Introduction: Other People's Wars . . . 5

1 Mounting Tensions 11

2 Superpower Rivalries and Proxy Warfare 29

3 The Faces of the Cold War 51

4 Negotiation and Innovation 73

5 The Legacy of Superpower Rivalries and Proxy Warfare 87

Chronology 101

Glossary 103

Bibliography 106

Further Information 108

Index 110

About the Author 112

The flags of the United States and the USSR represented very different governments and economic systems.

Other People's Wars

In 1945, World War II was drawing to a close. Germany surrendered in May, and in August, the United States detonated nuclear weapons over two Japanese cities, bringing the war in the Pacific to a close as well. It seemed as if a half century of wars—wars that involved very nearly the entire world—was at long last over, but the way that World War II ended set the tone for a new round of wars and new ways of fighting them.

The United States had only recently completed work on the nuclear weapons used against Japan. It was a shocking new technology, and once the world had seen the almost unbelievable destruction unleashed by atomic bombs, it was unthinkable that anyone would start another war and take the chance that these weapons might be used again. Only four years after the United States used its nuclear weapons, the Soviet Union developed its own. Many people thought that the very possibility of atomic warfare would mean the end of war. Sadly, it did not. However, a reluctance to use these powerful weapons most likely did prevent another war like the one that had just ended. What happened instead is an interesting and complex story.

After World War II, the political world was completely realigned, and two strong winners emerged: the United States and the Soviet Union. In Germany, the government, as well as the infrastructure and the economy, was in ruins, and it fell to these two victors, with help from their allies Great Britain and France, to fashion Germany into a functioning nation once more. It is unlikely that either the United States or the Soviet Union wanted to play this role in the world. For most of its history, the United States had done its best to keep to itself and let other nations handle their own affairs. The Soviet people had suffered tremendous losses in both world wars, and less than thirty years before, the nation had experienced a change in its own government when a Communist **coup** overthrew the Czar (emperor) of Russia and the Soviet Union was formed. Nonetheless, thanks to the strength of the United States economy and the strength of both nations' militaries, the two countries found themselves the two most powerful nations in a world that was badly in need of rebuilding. The arrangements made at this pivotal moment in history and the alliances that formed and dissolved would define much of the world for the next forty-five years.

The Soviet Union and the United States made an unlikely pair to team up as nation-builders—or rebuilders. Even though the United States and the Soviet Union had been reluctant allies in World War II, once their joint enemy, Germany, had been vanquished, it became obvious that their differences were greater than their commonalities. As we shall see in the coming chapters, the two new world powers had almost totally opposite beliefs about how society should be organized and about what kind of government was best. The United States was committed to **capitalism** while the Soviet Union was equally committed to **Communism**. Both nations wanted other countries to have the kinds of governments they approved of. The allies quickly turned into enemies.

Unfortunately, the enemies did not respond to the very real possibility of total nuclear annihilation by beating their swords, nuclear and otherwise, into ploughshares, and in the interest of world peace, attempting to get along no matter how great their differences. Instead, they nursed their ideological conflicts and jockeyed for power and influence around the world. Both nations attempted to reshape the world in accordance with their ideologies by supporting, in local conflicts and civil wars around the world, countries and factions that aligned with their belief systems. The United States backed capitalist regimes, and the Soviet Union backed Communist ones. The leaders of the two nations used **propaganda** to convince the populations of their countries as well as their allies in other countries of the importance of protecting the world from the other superpower—all the while building ever-increasing stockpiles of nuclear weapons in what became an arms race, with each superpower trying to make sure it had more weapons than the other.

The next forty-five years were by no means peaceful around the world. However, a world increasingly filled with weapons no one wanted to use prevented the unthinkable.

The Soviets often had public parades to show off their military, including missiles capable of carrying nuclear warheads.

Tensions eased and escalated over the years, but the superpowers were not unaware of the potential costs of a direct confrontation. Despite some tough talk and a couple of very close calls, the two countries never went to war directly. The United States never again used its nuclear weapons, and the Soviet Union never used the ones it built. In the end, the war remained primarily a war of ideas and ended at the negotiating table rather than on the battlefield. Because this war never turned nuclear and never got so far as direct battle between the two, it came to be known as the Cold War. The very "hot" wars around the world that the superpowers became involved in were called proxy wars because other nations or groups of fighters were fighting in their stead.

In the next chapter, you will learn more about the disagreements between these superpowers and how the Cold War got started. In chapter two, we will take a close look at the proxy wars and discover why and how they were fought and how they ended. In chapter three, you'll get to know some of the colorful personalities behind these many proxy wars over the years and learn about those frightening times when the world waited on edge to see if the superpowers were about to use nuclear weapons against one another. In chapter four, you'll learn what happened when the leaders finally did begin to negotiate and what technologies they developed along the way. In the closing chapter, we'll see what the world looked like after the end of the Cold War and how this unique approach to warfare changed the world.

Clement Atlee, Harry Truman, and Joseph Stalin met in Potsdam, Germany to make plans for postwar Europe.

CHAPTER ONE

Mounting Tensions

During World War II, the United States and the Soviet Union were allies in the effort to defeat Hitler and **fascism**. It was an odd alliance. The United States and the Soviet Union had a common enemy in Germany, but other than that, the two nations had deep ideological differences. Those differences went all the way back to 1917 and the Communist Revolution in Russia. When the Communist Party came to power and in 1922 formed the **USSR** (Union of Soviet Socialist Republics, also known as the Soviet Union), the United States refused to recognize the new nation. The Communist **ideology** of the Soviet Union promoted the idea that the collective good outweighed that of the individual, and both society and the economy were carefully managed and controlled by the government. The Communist government in the USSR abolished private property and free enterprise, severely limited the rights and freedoms of its people, and gave only lip service to free elections—all things that were abhorrent

Karl Marx

Karl Marx died thirty-four years before the Communist Revolution in Russia made way for the formation of the Soviet Union. But it was the work of Marx that inspired that revolution and all of modern Communism. Marx was born in Germany in 1818. When he grew up, he earned a Doctorate in Philosophy from the University of Jena in Germany. He worked for a time as a newspaper editor in Cologne, but then he moved to Paris, where he became immersed in **radical** ideas. In 1848, Marx published a pamphlet called *The Manifesto of the*

Karl Marx is widely considered one of the most influential thinkers in the history of the world.

Communist Party (or *The Communist Manifesto* as it is usually called today), which offered a succinct yet detailed critique of the class structure of Europe at that time, which Marx believed took advantage of the labor of workers for the benefit of the employers. He explains "the history of class struggles" in the opening of the manifesto:

> Freeman and slave, patrician and plebeian, lord and serf, guildmaster and journeyman, in a word, oppressor and oppressed, stood in constant opposition to one another, carried on an uninterrupted, now hidden, now open fight, that each time ended, either in the revolutionary reconstitution of society at large, or in the common ruin of the contending classes.

The manifesto called on workers to join together to change the social order, ending with the famous words, "Workers of the world, unite!"

When he was thirty-one, Marx moved to London, where he lived for the rest of his life. During those years, he wrote a great deal of political and economic philosophy. While he is considered the father of Communism, there has always been a lot of debate among Communists about the correct interpretation of his writings. The leader of the Communist Revolution in Russia was a man named Vladimir Lenin. His interpretations of Marx's thought became known as Marxist-Leninist philosophy and was the basis of the Soviet Union's ideology.

to the values that underpinned the United States. The United States was founded on and committed to principles of individual freedom, equality, private ownership of property and businesses, and capitalism. Thus, the United States was opposed to Communism on principle.

Despite these fundamental disagreements, however, the United States eventually recognized the USSR, and the two nations opened diplomatic relations in 1933. That happened largely because Russia needed military aid from the United States in order to fight Nazi Germany in World War II, and the United States very much wanted the Soviet Union to defeat the Nazis, hopefully without the United States having to enter the war. The United States did end up joining the war and worked with the Soviets to win it, but not before the German army had invaded the Soviet Union.

Soviet Distrust

The Soviet Union's problems with the United States were in some ways as practical as they were ideological. They suffered much more than the United States during World War II, losing more than twenty million people, not to mention a great deal of industry and farms. (The United States lost just over four hundred thousand soldiers and virtually no civilians.) Joseph Stalin, the leader of the USSR, was angry with the United States for waiting so long to confront the Germans in France. Had they done this sooner, he thought, it might have put enough pressure on the Germans on the Western European front to lessen the damage they were able to do to the Soviets.

The USSR was also concerned about the United States's new nuclear capabilities. President Harry Truman did not inform Stalin that the United States had developed an atomic bomb until July of 1945, when the Allied leaders met to discuss plans for the occupation of Germany after the war. Even though it is very likely that Soviet spies had already alerted Stalin to this development, the timing was not reassuring to the Soviet leader. It seemed as if Truman was trying to use the information that the United States had a nuclear bomb as leverage in the negotiations. In any case, the Soviet nuclear program was far behind that of the United States, and a nuclear-armed United States, particularly with Truman having been so secretive about its nuclear program, was very threatening to Stalin. Despite being allies in the fight against Nazi Germany, the two nations never became friendly, and events after the war only deepened their distrust of one another.

The two nations' ideological differences and cool relationship had not mattered so much before World War II, but afterwards, the balance of power in the world was totally realigned. The United States and the USSR emerged from the war as the two world superpowers. The United States economy had doubled during the war, and the United States was now the world's greatest industrial power. The Soviet economy was in very poor shape, and in addition, much of the country had been laid to waste by the German invasion. In addition to the millions of Soviet citizens who had died in the war, almost as many were homeless and hungry after the war. But despite this, the Soviet Union still had the world's largest army. After the devastation the Soviet Union had suffered at the hands of the German army, the Soviets were determined to use that military to make sure it was never again invaded from the West. The United States, for its part, feared the expansion of Soviet influence into Western Europe—with good reason, as it would turn out. The war left the economies and infrastructures of the other countries in Western Europe a disaster as well. Rebuilding Europe would take a lot of work, and the Soviet Union and the United States had very different ideas for how to go about that.

An Iron Curtain

During the war, the Soviet army had invaded many Eastern Europe countries that Hitler had taken over. Stalin promised the Allies that after the war these countries would be free, but he went back on that promise almost immediately. Stalin had deep fears of Germany regaining any sort of power. This was understandable considering how much suffering the Germany army had inflicted upon his country. In an attempt to protect itself from yet another military invasion from the West, the Soviet Union created between itself and Western Europe a buffer zone of countries that were ideologically sympathetic and militarily dependent on the Soviet Union. These countries—Poland, Albania, Bulgaria, Hungary, Romania, and Czechoslovakia—came to be known as the Eastern Bloc. These governments were called "puppet governments," because even though they were officially independent, they were ruled by people chosen by and loyal to the Soviet Union, and the USSR used its military to maintain control of these countries. The people were not

President Truman waves his hat, and Prime Minister Churchill flashes the Victory sign, as they head to Westminster College where Churchill will deliver his famous iron curtain speech.

allowed to choose their own leaders or to have a say in the laws and policies of their governments. This was, of course, contrary to the commitment of the United States and the countries of Western Europe to democracy and freedom.

This border of countries controlled by the Soviet Union stretched across Europe and effectively divided it into two parts—one free, one not; one aligned with the Soviet Union, and one aligned with the United States and Western Europe. In a speech in 1946, Winston Churchill, who had been prime minister of Britain during the war, described this situation by saying that, "an iron curtain has descended across the continent." Stalin responded by calling Churchill a "firebrand of war" and asking, "What can be surprising in the fact that the Soviet Union, in a desire to ensure its security for the future, tries to achieve that these countries should have governments whose relations to the Soviet Union are loyal?"

Despite the lack of freedom and self-government in the Eastern Bloc nations, many people in Western European countries suffering from post-war poverty were attracted to the Communist ideology, with its government support of industry and common ownership of the nation's wealth. Communist parties were strong in France, Italy, and Greece. This added to the concerns of the leaders of the United States and Britain that Soviet ideology and perhaps even Soviet rule would spread to the rest of the continent.

Changes in Policy

Prior to World War II, the United States had a policy of avoiding conflicts that did not directly involve the United

States. That changed in 1947 with the Truman Doctrine, a commitment by the United States to provide political, economic, and most disturbingly to the USSR, military assistance to any democratic nation that was facing a threat of authoritarian rule—either from an outside force or from armed factions within the country. The ramifications of this

President Truman signs the National Security Act of 1947.

policy would have effects around the world. In addition, as a part of the new foreign policy approach, the United States passed the National Security Act of 1947. This legislation reorganized the authority structure of the military and foreign policy establishment and gave more power to the president and his immediate advisors to pursue foreign policy agendas. The National Security Act created the Central Intelligence Agency (CIA), a spying organization that would gather information and, in many cases, interfere in the affairs of other nations. The CIA would be used extensively in the many wars to come over the next four decades. Then in 1949, the United States, Canada, and ten European nations formed the North Atlantic Treaty Organization (NATO), an alliance in which the member countries agreed to provide military support in case of an armed attack against any one member. Clearly, this was intended to strengthen the member nations against any potential aggression by the Soviet Union. All of this served only to increase the Soviet Union's distrust of the United States. (The Eastern Bloc would respond in 1955 by creating the Warsaw Pact, a similar military alliance that put the Soviet Union in command of any military campaigns engaged in by Warsaw Pact member nations.)

A Divided Country

In 1945, in Germany, the two new superpowers faced each other more directly. The leaders of the victorious nations, Stalin, Truman, and Churchill, met in Potsdam, Germany to work out a plan for post-war Europe, particularly Germany. (Churchill was replaced during the two-week meeting by

Berlin Wall

Because the Western allies were putting more money into the Western sectors of Germany, wages were higher, and there was a higher standard of living in the West than in the East. Between 1949 and 1961, more than two million people left East Germany to live in the West, many of them escaping by traveling to East Berlin and then crossing to the western side of the city.

Many of these people were educated and skilled workers, such as engineers, doctors, and teachers. Losing these workers made it even harder for East Germany to improve its economy. In 1961, Soviet leader Nikita Khrushchev, who had come to power shortly after Stalin died in 1953, demanded that the United States give over their control of West Berlin. In June of that year, United States president John Kennedy flew to Berlin and made a powerful speech assuring the people of West Berlin that the United States would not abandon them. *"Ich bin ein Berliner,"* he said, meaning "I am a Berliner," indicating solidarity with the people of Berlin.

Khrushchev did not let it rest, however. On the morning of August 13, the people of Berlin awoke to find a barrier of barbed wire stretched across their city, and armed troops guarding the border. Within a few weeks, there was a wall around the entire city that was fifteen feet (4.6 meters) high, separating East from West. It became the most visible symbol of the oppression of Communist governments. It would be another twenty-eight years before the people of East Berlin could travel freely to the West.

Germany's infrastructure and economy were devastated by World War II.

the incoming prime minister, Clement Attlee.) In what was meant to be a temporary measure, the Allies divided Germany into four zones. The Americans, the British, and the French administered the Western two-thirds of the country, and the Soviets were responsible for the Eastern third. Germany's capital, Berlin, was in the Soviet zone. Berlin was meant to be administered jointly by the four powers but was divided into four separate sectors for administrative purposes. The idea was for each of the victors to aid and support their part of the country in rebuilding and reestablishing democracy and self-government, but the differences between the ruling powers led to a line being drawn across Germany as well. Just as the iron curtain was dividing Europe into a pro-Soviet part and a pro-Western part, Germany was soon divided into two completely different states. East Germany (German Democratic Republic) had a Communist government, supported and controlled by the Soviets. West Germany (Federal Republic of Germany) was an independent capitalist nation aided and supported by the United States and Britain. The Soviet sector of Berlin became known as East Berlin, and the rest of the city was known as West Berlin. The lines had been drawn across Europe—and right through the middle of Berlin—with the United States on one side and the Soviet Union on the other.

Indirect War

By 1949, the United States had built up a small arsenal of nuclear weapons in Europe, specifically to deter the Soviets from moving further west. Then in 1949, the Allies discovered that the Soviet Union had developed its own nuclear weapons. The two most powerful nations in the world were facing each other in Europe, each with an arsenal of the most powerful weapons ever made, and they regarded each other with increasing distrust and dislike. It was not a comfortable situation.

However, neither Truman nor Stalin was especially concerned about the possibility of nuclear war. It's possible

Ionizing radiation moves through the atmosphere after a 1946 nuclear bomb test at Bikini Atoll in Micronesia.

that had the two superpowers not possessed nuclear weapons, the tensions between them would have boiled over into another conventional war, right on the heels of the Second World War. Though the two nations stood at the brink of war, each knew that if a war started, nuclear weapons would likely be used. And if nuclear weapons were used, both countries would be annihilated. Despite the power of having these weapons, no one wanted to use them. This stalemate came to be known as the Cold War because though it lasted for the next forty-five years, the two nations never went to war with each other directly. That is not to say that the conflict between the two never led to a "hot" war. Sadly, it did. The rival superpowers engaged in many proxy wars on several continents. A proxy war is a war in which two powers—in this case the United States and the USSR—do not directly engage in combat but provide support in the form of weapons, financial aid, and other types of assistance to opposing sides of the conflict, in effect going to war with each other indirectly. By engaging in proxy wars, there was less risk of the two nuclear powers actually using their nuclear weapons, because though the superpowers supplied arms to the sides they supported, they did not share their nuclear arsenals with the countries they backed. These proxy wars were for the most part far from Europe. Over the four-and-a-half decades that the Cold War lasted, the Soviet Union and the United States carried on proxy wars in Central and South America, Africa, the Middle East, and Central and Southeast Asia. In these places, the Cold War got very hot indeed. Millions of people in many different countries, and soldiers of both the United States and the Soviet Union, died in or as a result of these many wars.

Though the ideological differences mentioned above—the commitment of the United States to individual freedom and free-enterprise capitalism, and the commitment of the USSR to the tenets of Communism and state controlled economics—were fundamentally at the root of the conflict between the superpowers, as with all such conflicts, the stakes of these proxy wars came to be as much about resources, power, and alliances, as ideology. Each nation wanted to expand its sphere of influence and protect the influence it already had. As we shall see in coming chapters, the many proxy wars of the Cold War were complex and difficult to analyze, and in the end, the reasons for these wars were often very unclear.

Propaganda posters, like this one of Vladimir Lenin, were common in the Soviet Union.

CHAPTER TWO

Superpower Rivalries and Proxy Warfare

After the dust had settled at the end of World War II, the United States and the Soviet Union, former allies and now adversaries, found themselves in conflict with each other in hot spots around the world. The two nations had vastly different ideologies, and both were committed to containing the spread of the other's worldview. However, the countries they backed in these proxy wars had their own ideologies and ambitions as well, and these were not always perfectly aligned with those of whichever superpower backed them. While it is important to understand that at the root of these conflicts is the stark contrast between free market capitalism, staunchly supported by the United States, and Marxist-Leninist Communism, just as staunchly supported by the USSR, these were not the only issues deciding what nation or faction each superpower supported in these indirect conflicts. A strong fear of the other power gaining too much influence in a region often led to some rather strange alliances. For example, in Latin

America, the United States was all too willing to abandon its commitment to democracy and support a dictator if that democracy was likely to result in a Communist government and the dictator would resist it.

The objectives, concerns, and motivations were different in each of the places where the superpowers confronted each other. In some cases, the threat to one nation or the other was obvious, such as in Cuba. In others, such as Vietnam, the motivations were trickier to understand. A closer look at the places and situations where proxy wars were fought will provide a picture of a world where alliances were as complex as the ideologies that led to those alliances. Through it all was the realization that if ever these two nuclear powers did come into direct conflict, the fate of the entire world would lie in the balance.

Civil War in Greece

In the first proxy war between the United States and the Soviet Union, neither superpower actually sent any troops. Even before World War II was over, Greece, who had joined the Allies in 1940, was dealing with its own internal strife, a civil war in which various groups fought to gain and maintain power. By 1947, the Greek Communist Party, backed by Albania, Yugoslavia, and Bulgaria (all countries that were allied to the Soviet Union), was trying to take power from the current Greek government that had been backed by Britain. However, Britain, still recovering from World War I, did not have the resources to continue to be of much help. Britain asked the United States to step in and support the Greek government. The United States was more than willing. In fact, it was in a speech requesting aid for Greece's civil war that Truman first outlined the Truman Doctrine. The United States made no secret of the fact that it was supporting the Greek government, not solely to end the tragedy of a civil war that was unfolding there, nor because of any particular commonality with the government itself, but in order to stop the spread of Communism. In his request for Greek aid, Truman said, "The free peoples of the world look to us for support in maintaining their freedoms." The message was not lost on Stalin. This was a more comprehensive plan than merely stepping in to help Britain help Greece. The United States was allying itself with all "free peoples," however the United States defined them.

In an earlier agreement with Great Britain, the USSR had pledged to not support Communist forces in Greece in exchange for being allowed control of the governments in Eastern Europe. It worked well for Stalin; he could maintain control of the nations of Eastern Europe, and if necessary, support the rebels in Greece. With the considerable financial help of the United States, however, the Greek Communists were defeated by the summer of 1949. Meanwhile, conflicts were stirring in other parts of the world, and the superpowers would send guns and money—and many, many troops.

Trouble in Korea

The end of the war left things very unsettled in Asia as well. Prior to World War II, the small nation of Korea had been a part of the Japanese Empire. When the United

One of the most famous latitude lines in history, the thirty-eighth parallel, divided Korea into two nations.

States defeated Japan, Korea found itself suddenly free. Most Koreans wanted a unified state, but the superpowers didn't give them a choice. In 1948, they divided the country along the thirty-eighth **parallel**. In the north, the Soviets supported a Communist regime led by Kim Il-Sung, who had trained and fought with the Soviet Army in World War II and returned to Korea from the Soviet Union only in 1945. In the south, the United States supported a democratic government led by Syngman Rhee. In June of 1950, after securing support from Communist China as well as the Soviet Union, Soviet tanks carried Kim's forces across the thirty-eighth parallel into South Korea in an attempt to unify the nation under Communist rule. This was the beginning of the Korean War.

The Korean War was not a matter of one nation attempting to take over another but of a divided nation trying to reunite. The United States had not provided South Korea with offensive weapons because it feared that if it did, South Korea would invade the north. The two governments were bitterly opposed, but both wanted a unified nation. Truman, however, saw the invasion of South Korea as a first step in a Soviet-led Communist takeover of the world, and as his chance to declare war on Communism itself. The United States, along with nineteen other United Nations (UN) countries, sent troops to help the South fight off the invading armies from the North, making the Korean War the first major proxy war of the Cold War. (Though sixteen of the nineteen UN countries sent some soldiers, the United States provided ninety percent of the troops that aided South Korea throughout the war.)

The United States intervention in Korea was in keeping with the Truman Doctrine as well as with NSC-68, a then top-secret document of the United States National Security Council. NSC-68 called for the "containment" of Soviet influence, but the wording of the document seems a bit more aggressive than the word "containment" suggests. "It is clear," the document reads, "that a substantial and rapid building up of strength in the free world is necessary to

Red Scare

During the 1950s, Americans were concerned that the Soviet Union would try to take over the United States. Though this was highly unlikely, these fears reached ludicrous proportions, with often devastating results for the individuals involved.

Some members of the United States government aided and abetted these fears, most famously, Joseph McCarthy, a United States senator from Wisconsin. McCarthy used gossip, rumor, and **innuendo** to accuse hundreds of people of supporting a Communist takeover of the United States. Though McCarthy rarely had any evidence for his claims, he stirred up panic and

With very little evidence but a great deal of showmanship, Senator Joseph McCarthy whipped up anti-Communist paranoia during the 1950s.

paranoia among the American people. In addition to McCarthy's investigations, a committee of the United States House of Representatives, called the House Un-American Activities Committee (HUAC), was **convened** to investigate people who had been accused of being Communist sympathizers. A *New York Times* report about McCarthy's hearings describes how McCarthy suddenly accused one of the defense lawyers, Joseph Welch, of having Communist ties. According to the *New York Times*, "Mr. Welch, almost in tears from this unexpected attack, told the Wisconsin Republican that 'until this moment, Senator, I think I never really gauged your cruelty or your recklessness.'"

Those who had been accused often found it difficult to get and keep jobs. The committee put a special focus on the entertainment industry. Many writers, directors, and actors were blacklisted, which meant they weren't allowed to work on films because of unsubstantiated allegations that they were anti-American. Before cooler heads in Congress brought this "Red Scare" to an end, the lives and careers of many innocent people had been ruined.

support a firm policy intended to check and to roll back the **Kremlin's** drive for world domination." The United States's aim was not merely to contain but to counter with a spread of its own ideology and "roll back" gains the Kremlin had already made.

It is not clear, however, that in Korea at least, the Soviet Union was bent on world domination. Stalin didn't initially try to get control of the entire Korean peninsula but merely seemed to want to keep the factions there in balance. In the discussions among the Allies after World War II, Stalin made no demands about Korea and went along with whatever plans Truman suggested for the country. However, it was in the interests of the Soviet Union that North Korea, at least, be in the hands of a Soviet-friendly government. An invasion of the Asian continent by means of Korea could put hostile interests at the back door of the USSR. So when it became clear that Kim would invade the South with or without Soviet backing, the Soviets supported him rather than take the chance that the South would win.

Though the North had some early victories, and even took Seoul, the South Korean capital, their incursion didn't last long. US General Douglas MacArthur led the coalition in the South, and using the US Navy and Air Force as well as ground troops, pushed the North Korean forces back to the thirty-eighth parallel—and in fact a bit beyond the thirty-eighth and into North Korean territory. The leader of Communist China, Mao Zedong, was alarmed by this, fearing that United States troops planned to move into China. He responded by sending hundreds of thousands

The Vietnam Memorial in Washington, DC, lists the names of more than 58,000 Americans who lost their lives in the Vietnam war.

of Chinese soldiers pouring across the border into Korea to attack the US-led troops and force them back into the South.

MacArthur wanted to invade China and use nuclear weapons against the North Koreans, but Truman refused to authorize it, and a nuclear war was avoided in this first proxy war to involve United States and Soviet troops. In 1953, open fighting was stopped in a cease-fire, but a peace treaty was never signed, and technically the Korean War is still not over. The country remains divided. Over the three years of fighting more than five million people, both soldiers and civilians, died in the Korean War.

The Long Vietnam War

In the 1940s, while World War II was raging in Europe, in southeast Asia, Vietnam was fighting France for its independence. France had colonized Vietnam after World War I but was too weakened from World War II to continue to administer and control its colonies. Communist forces in the northern part of the country, led by Ho Chi Minh, wrested power from the French in 1954. An agreement made for the withdrawal of France from the country divided Vietnam along the seventeenth parallel. Ho's Communist government was in charge of the North, and in the South, factions who had backed France were in charge, though the government there was not a democracy. There were to be general elections in 1956 to reunite the country. However, the United States, seeing that the Communists were likely to win, did not agree to nationwide elections, but instead held elections just in the South. Dinh Diem was elected, but nationalist forces loyal to the North, a group called the Vietcong, began a **guerrilla war** in an attempt to reunite the country under the government of the North.

In 1965, the United States began a huge build-up of troops and a sustained bombing campaign in Vietnam. This marked the beginning of what in the United States was called the Vietnam War, and in Vietnam, the American War (though the United States had had special forces there for many years). As with Korea, the conflict was not a matter of one country trying to take over another. Rather, the conflict was an internal dispute with factions within Vietnam wanting to reunite the country but disagreeing on what form of government should be in charge. However, in the case of Vietnam, it was fairly clear that if left to themselves, the Communists would come out victorious. United States involvement in Vietnam was due mostly to the United States' fear of what was known as the domino theory, or the idea that when one country fell to a Communist government, others in the region would follow, leading to Soviet control of entire regions of the world.

The Soviet Union supported the North Vietnamese and the Vietcong with both economic and military aid. However, they had ideological differences with China, which was also supporting the Vietcong, as well as with the United States. The existing differences about Communist ideology between the USSR and Communist China had only deepened over the years. The Soviet Union wanted to limit the influence of the Chinese in southeast Asia as much as they wanted to limit American influence.

China

Although the main antagonists in the Cold War were the United States and the Soviet Union, China played a role, too. In 1949, Communists under the leadership of Mao Zedong, took over the government of China. Neither Washington nor Moscow interfered very much with the change in power in China, though the United States did provide some economic aid in support of the government and made a diplomatic effort to prevent a civil war. These efforts were unsuccessful, however, and Mao quickly consolidated power.

This might have made strong allies of the USSR and China in an attempt to spread Communism around the world, except for the fact that what were now the two largest Communist governments in the world had significant differences in their interpretation of Communism. Mao's brand of Communism was very different from the USSR's Marxist-Leninist version, and the two nations' leaders rarely saw eye-to-eye. Mao got along well enough with Stalin, but when Stalin died in 1953 and was replaced by Nikita Khrushchev, relations between the two Communist countries grew worse.

Though, like the Soviets, the Chinese wanted the United States out of Korea and Vietnam, they also wanted to be sure that the USSR didn't end up with too much influence in southeast Asia. In the end, China and the USSR were often competing as much with each other for influence as they were competing with the United States.

By 1968, it was becoming increasingly clear that a military solution to the conflict was unlikely. The war was proving very expensive to both the superpowers, and the United States was rapidly losing support for the war at home. Both the United States and the Soviet Union wanted to end the war, but it proved difficult to come to terms that suited everyone. As relations between the United States and China improved, and the Soviet Union saw hope for easing the tensions between themselves and the United States, both superpowers began to search for a way out of the conflict. A peace settlement was eventually reached in 1973, and two years later the north Vietnamese invaded south Vietnam and the country became a single Communist nation. It remains so today. More than three million people, two million of them civilians, died in the Vietnam War.

Central America: Too Close to Home

The Korean and Vietnam Wars were major wars, one of which lasted most of a decade, but in Central America, the proxy wars took a slightly more subtle character—at least from the point of view of the superpowers. In Latin America, Washington and Moscow were often involved in clandestine support for revolutionary factions, and rather than stepping in once civil wars had begun, they often instigated such wars in attempts to bring down governments they did not like. In order to set the stage for the many conflicts in Latin America during the 1970s and 1980s, we need to go back to the early 1960s in Cuba.

On January 1, 1959, the dictator of the island nation of Cuba was overthrown by revolutionary forces led by Fidel Castro. Within the year, the new Cuban government had seized private property, **nationalized** many businesses (including many US-owned sugar plantations), and imposed heavy taxes on goods imported from the United States. Washington responded by placing restrictions on trade with Cuba. Castro then asked for and received a great deal of both economic and military aid from Moscow. Castro proclaimed himself a Marxist-Leninist and allied his nation with the USSR. This prompted President Eisenhower to cut off all diplomatic relations with Cuba.

On October 16, 1962, President John Kennedy was shown photographs, taken from United States spy planes, of Soviet missile sites on the island of Cuba—a mere ninety miles (144.8 kilometers) from the United States coast. There had been no indication that either of the superpowers had any intention of using nuclear weapons against each other, but both sides had been beefing up their nuclear arsenals. Now Soviet missiles were in the United States's backyard.

Castro's embrace of Soviet missiles may have been in part a retaliation for an attempt in April of 1961 by the United States to remove him from power. The CIA had trained Cuban exiles to invade Cuba and overthrow Castro's government, promising support during the invasion. When the invaders landed at the Bay of Pigs in Cuba, the promised help did not arrive, and the revolutionaries were killed or captured. While the Bay of Pigs invasion was not a direct action of aggression toward the Soviet Union, it was a clear

Surveillance photographs clearly show Soviet missile installations in Cuba.

indication that the United States was willing to interfere in nations that allied themselves with the Soviets, increasing the Soviets' distrust of the United States.

Kennedy, who had been in office less than two years, found himself dealing with what was perhaps the greatest crisis in world history. Sending the United States military to destroy the missile sites could lead to nuclear war. Not destroying the missile sites left open the very real possibility of a nuclear strike on the United States. Ships with nuclear bombs to arm the missiles were already on their way to Cuba from the USSR. So Kennedy surrounded the island with United States warships to prevent any shipments from the Soviets from getting in. Then he talked with Khrushchev. Khrushchev seemed to be taking a hard line, but after thirteen tense days, the two leaders came to an agreement. The Soviets would remove the missile sites, and the United States promised not to invade Cuba and agreed to remove missiles that it had in Turkey. The ships carrying the warheads turned home, and the threat of nuclear war had passed for the time being.

Despite the close call in Cuba, both sides continued to engage in proxy wars in Latin America. The United States emerged from its confrontation with the Soviets in Cuba determined to prevent other Latin American countries—countries that were, figuratively speaking, in the United States's backyard—from becoming allied with the USSR. While the United States claimed to support democratically elected governments, it in fact supported brutal dictatorships as long as they were anti-Communist. Democratically elected governments in Latin America, such as those in Guatemala, the Dominican Republic, and Chile, for example, were thought to be too supportive of Communist ideology, so the United States supported their overthrow, primarily by providing weapons and funds and training soldiers to carry out military coups against these governments. As George Kennan, the American diplomat who developed the United States policy of containment put it, "it is better to have a strong regime in power than a liberal one if [the

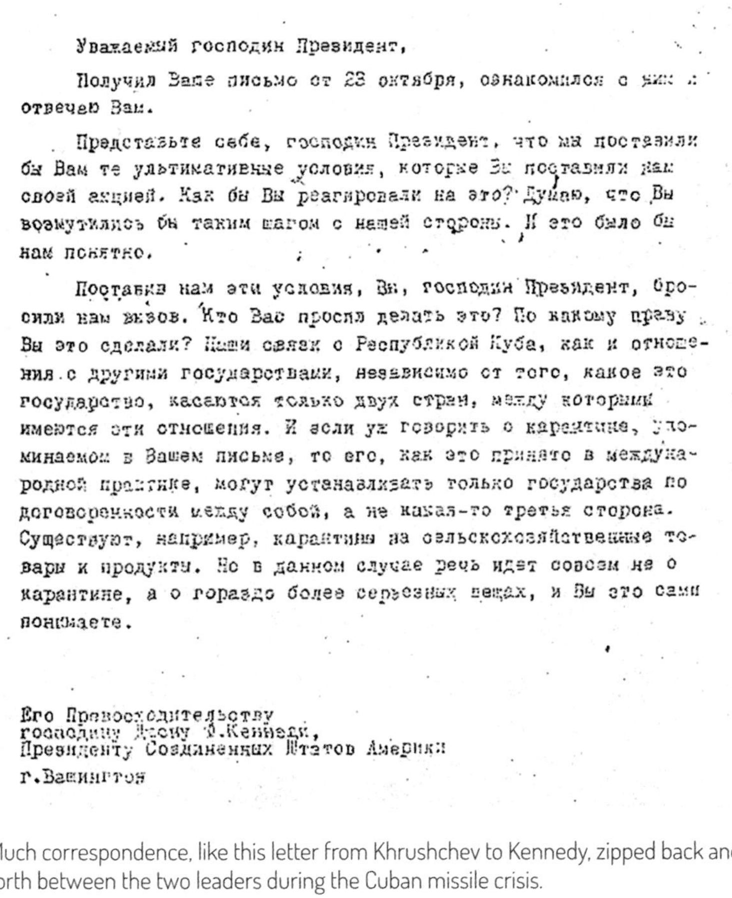

Уважаемый господин Президент,

Получил Ваше письмо от 23 октября, ознакомился с ним и отвечаю Вам.

Представьте себе, господин Президент, что мы поставили бы Вам те ультимативные условия, которые Вы поставили нам своей акцией. Как бы Вы реагировали на это? Думаю, что Вы возмутились бы таким шагом с нашей стороны. И это было бы нам понятно.

Поставив нам эти условия, Вы, господин Президент, бросили нам вызов. Кто Вас просил делать это? По какому праву Вы это сделали? Наши связи с Республикой Куба, как и отношения с другими государствами, независимо от того, какое это государство, касаются только двух стран, между которыми имеются эти отношения. И если уж говорить о карантине, упоминаемом в Вашем письме, то его, как это принято в международной практике, могут устанавливать только государства по договоренности между собой, а не какая-то третья сторона. Существуют, например, карантины на сельскохозяйственные товары и продукты. Но в данном случае речь идет совсем не о карантине, а о гораздо более серьезных вещах, и Вы это сами понимаете.

Его Превосходительству
господину Джону Ф.Кеннеди,
Президенту Соединенных Штатов Америки
г.Вашингтон

Much correspondence, like this letter from Khrushchev to Kennedy, zipped back and forth between the two leaders during the Cuban missile crisis.

liberal one] is indulgent and relaxed and penetrated by Communists." Because of the poverty and inequality under these dictatorships, and because the people were getting no help from the United States to relieve this burden, they were often attracted to Marxist ideology with its emphasis on social and economic equality and elimination of class distinctions. The Soviet Union saw this as an opportunity to increase its influence in the Americas and give economic and military aid, either directly or through Cuba, to many of the armed revolutionaries.

Struggles in the Middle East and Africa

The two superpowers were also in conflict in the Middle East during the Cold War. But here, there was more at stake for the superpowers than ideology. By the end of World War II, oil had become one of the world's most valued resources, and the Middle East had much of the world's oil supply.

The conflicts in the Middle East, particularly those between Israel and Palestine, have deep and complex roots distinct from the ideologies of the Cold War. However, because of the strategic importance of this oil-rich region, the United States and the Soviet Union sought influence over the various governments there. When the nation of Israel was formed in 1948, the United States provided an enormous amount of military and economic aid, even though that meant alienating many of the Arab states in the region, especially Palestine. In turn, the USSR gave

The last Soviet tanks rolled out of Afghanistan in 1989.

economic and military aid to nations, such as Syria and Egypt, and independent groups, such as the Palestinian Liberation Army (PLO), that were committed to the destruction of Israel.

Africa also provided battlegrounds in the proxy wars of the superpowers. European nations that had colonized much of Africa pulled out of the region in the 1950s and 1960s, and many new African countries were formed. Again, each of the superpowers was concerned that the other would gain power in the region, and thus sought to secure allies among the newly independent African nations who were struggling to form solid and lasting governments. Military aid from both of the superpowers flowed to rebel groups in many African countries as the superpowers vied to maintain an upper hand in the region.

Afghanistan: The Last of the Proxy Wars

One of the last places where the Soviet Union and the United States fought a proxy war during the Cold War was in Afghanistan, a country that shared a border with the Soviet Union. In 1978, a Communist government took over Afghanistan. A civil war erupted because the new government was not popular with many of the Afghan people, primarily because it was not friendly to Islam, the nation's main religion. In December of 1979, the Soviet Union invaded the country with thousands of troops and took military control of the capital in order to make sure that a Soviet-friendly government stayed in power.

The United States loudly denounced the Soviet invasion and secretly supported rebels who were fighting against the Soviet-backed government. The conflict wore on, and the Soviet Union became more and more embroiled in the war. The cost in lives and money was a tremendous drain on the Soviets. The USSR's involvement in Afghanistan has often been compared to the United States' involvement in Vietnam—many years of death and wasted resources in a war that could not be won. In 1989, ten years after the invasion, Mikhail Gorbachev, the new reformist leader of the Soviet Union, removed all Soviet troops from Afghanistan and ended the last of the proxy wars of the Cold War.

Joseph Stalin and Harry Truman were the first two architects of the Cold War.

CHAPTER THREE

The Faces of the Cold War

The story of the Cold War is one of ideological disagreements and often uncertain alliances, of an arms race and many bloody wars. But behind the political maneuverings of these bellicose years is a cast of colorful characters. Here is a look at a few of the men behind forty-five years of proxy warfare.

Douglas MacArthur

Douglas MacArthur was the son of an army officer who had fought for the United States Army during the United States Civil War and received a Congressional Medal of Honor for his bravery. He had always wanted to grow up to be a military hero like his dad. In 1898, he was accepted into the United States Military Academy at West Point, where he graduated first in his class. By the time the United States entered World War I in 1917, MacArthur was a colonel and in charge of a division, and by the end of the war he was a

Douglas MacArthur was a talented and bold—though often headstrong—general.

Brigadier General and the most decorated American soldier in that war. In World War II, he was commander of the Pacific forces, and at the end of the war, he was in charge of rebuilding Japan.

When the Korean War began, MacArthur was one of the most respected—and most famous—military leaders in the United States, and he was put in charge of protecting the South Koreans from an invasion by the North Koreans. MacArthur had not become the successful military leader he was by being timid and cautious. In fact, he was known for being bold. This had worked beautifully when fighting the Japanese, but he miscalculated in Korea. MacArthur attacked the North Koreans at a point north of the thirty-eighth parallel, the line that divided North Korea from South Korea. China responded by sending troops over the border into Korea to help the North Koreans. President Truman had ordered MacArthur not to take the battle into China, but MacArthur saw his soldiers being killed by the Chinese army, and he wanted to respond rather than withdraw. He even wanted to use nuclear weapons against North Korea. The disagreement between Truman and MacArthur, who was a great hero back home, became public, and MacArthur had a great deal of support. But in the end, Truman won. He relieved MacArthur of his command. MacArthur retired from the army and spent his retirement writing his memoirs.

Harry S. Truman

Harry Truman became the president of the United States during World War II, after the sudden death of Franklin Delano Roosevelt, for whom Truman served as Vice President. Truman and Roosevelt had not been close, and Roosevelt had shared few details of foreign affairs with his vice president. Truman had to make some very difficult decisions—such as to use atomic weapons against Japan—with very little experience on the job. However, it was the decisions he made after the end of World War II that in many ways determined the course of history throughout the Cold War.

Truman's policies, such as the Truman Doctrine and the policy of containment, reflect a deep fear of the spread of Communism and a desire to block the influence of the Soviet Union in any way he could. In order to advance this agenda, Truman maneuvered to make changes in the way foreign policy was conducted in Washington so that the president and his advisors would have much more independence from Congress than they had previously. Truman likely felt a strong need to control events considering the world situation he found when he came to office.

Why he was so staunchly opposed to Communism is less clear. Truman grew up poor on a farm in Missouri. There was no money for college, so he worked at many different jobs after high school. He served in the military in World War I, and after a failed attempt at running a hat store, became involved in politics, where he finally found success. Truman was deeply in debt after the failure of his business, but he refused to accept offers of bankruptcy protection. He paid off all the debt even though it took him many years. Perhaps his experience with making his way without much help instilled in him a passion for free enterprise even though his experience with it wasn't particularly successful. It is also possible that his hatred of Communism was due to his experience with, and knowledge of, Joseph Stalin rather than any particular ideological features of Marxist-Leninist theory.

Joseph Stalin

Joseph Stalin came to power in the USSR upon the death of Vladimir Lenin, who had led the Communist Revolution there. Stalin built a strong military, the **Red Army**, that helped defeat Hitler. At home, Stalin was a powerful and brutal dictator. His approach to creating a Communist society was to impose the principles of Communism, such as **collectivization** of industry and agriculture, by force. The rapid and coercive nature of these economic changes, particularly to agriculture, resulted in a famine in which millions of people died. Stalin was able to hold onto power despite the difficult conditions in his country because he imprisoned or executed anyone who was even suspected of opposing him or his programs. In Stalin's version of Communism, the people might technically own the nation's wealth, but they had no say whatsoever about how that wealth was used or distributed.

Oddly, Stalin did not seem as determined to spread Communism around the world as Truman and his advisors seemed to think. Stalin was, however, deeply suspect of the United States and the nations of Western Europe, and when he learned that the United States had developed nuclear weapons, he began an intense effort to catch up with the Americans' nuclear program. Thanks to the virtually unlimited financial support of the government, Soviet scientists were able to develop an atomic bomb much faster than the United States had expected, getting their first nuclear weapon in 1949, and an arms race between the two nations soon began.

The Berlin Blockade

The Soviet Union and the United States never quite fought a proxy war in Berlin, but that city was both the birthplace of the Cold War and the place where its first serious crisis played out. In 1948, when the other allies began to introduce policies that would help Germany become an independent nation once again, the Soviets became concerned that Germany might become too powerful and invade them yet another time. They responded by imposing a blockade on West Berlin, preventing any supplies from getting into the city from the West. (Recall that the western sector of the city was completely surrounded by Soviet-controlled East Germany.) Without supplies of food, the two-and-a-half million people who lived in the western sectors of the city were at risk of starving. Though some of Truman's advisors advocated giving in to Stalin and pulling out of Berlin, Truman was adamant, saying, "We stay in Berlin—period." The West responded immediately with a plan code-named "Operation Vittles" to airlift supplies into the city.

The blockade backfired on the Soviets. Rather than interfering with the establishment of an independent Germany, the blockade spurred the other allies into making it happen sooner. It also convinced the West that the Soviet Union was indeed a threat to democratic government and contributed to the establishment of the NATO (North Atlantic Treaty Organization). Stalin lifted the blockade in 1949, but the damage had been done. The first crisis of the Cold War had been averted, but not without long-lasting effects.

Much of Stalin's decision-making during the proxy wars seemed designed more to protect the Soviet Union's buffer zones, as in Afghanistan, or to keep a balance of influence in more far-flung parts of the world. It was not until Stalin died in 1953 and Nikita Khrushchev came to power that the Soviets seemed as bent on the spread of world Communism as the rest of the world had been saying they were.

Nikita Khrushchev

When Nikita Khrushchev became leader of the Soviet Union after the death of Joseph Stalin, it seemed likely that he would be a much more moderate leader, perhaps softening the tensions between the two superpowers. He spoke openly about Stalin's crimes and began a process called "de-Stalinization." He freed many people Stalin had imprisoned and somewhat eased restrictions on dissent. It looked like Khrushchev might be willing to work with his rival superpower.

However, in 1956, not long after he came to power, he responded to an uprising against the Communist government of Hungary by sending troops and tanks to make sure the country stayed under Soviet control. In 1961, his government helped to build the Berlin Wall. In 1962, he sent nuclear weapons to Cuba, precipitating the Cuban Missile Crisis. Khrushchev was proving to be an even more formidable opponent than Stalin had been.

Khrushchev had been born into a poor peasant family, and only because of the Communist revolution was he able to get technical education that offered him a chance for

Nikita Khrushchev was one of the most colorful of a cast of many colorful Cold War leaders.

a better life. He was deeply committed to the beliefs and goals of Communism. He believed that the Communist approach to economics and way of life would eventually win over capitalism because it was truly a better system. His support for Communist countries in Africa and Latin America often included providing funds for dams and stadiums—not just armies.

He was a colorful figure, bragging about his country's achievements and pulling public relations stunts, such as having his country be the first to put a dog in space. He may be best remembered for an incident at a United Nations meeting in New York, where a delegate from the Philippines accused the Soviet Union of swallowing up Eastern Europe and denying civil rights to the people there. Khrushchev reportedly leapt to his feet, pulled off his shoe, and waved it in the air. Then, he banged it on the table as he disputed the charge.

His antics weren't popular at home, though, and he lost a great deal of respect from his countrymen over the Cuban Missile Crisis. Thanks to his reforms, which were not popular with the more conservative element of the party, his political opponents were able to replace him two years later through peaceful, if coercive, means.

John F. Kennedy

If the Cuban Missile Crisis was the low point in Khrushchev's career, it was quite the opposite for President John Kennedy. Kennedy was the opposite of Khrushchev in other ways as well. He had grown up in an extremely wealthy family and attended the best schools. He was also groomed by his family for a career in politics.

However, he was a new and untried leader when the Cuban Missile Crisis erupted in 1962, having taken office less than two years before. He was also young—not quite forty-five years old at the time. Nevertheless, he managed that difficult situation well and presumably with nerves of steel. However, he suffered a great deal of criticism for the Bay of Pigs debacle and for letting the world get that close to a nuclear war.

Kennedy's hardline anti-Communist stance was no surprise. While campaigning for president, he promised to strengthen the military and make a tough stand against Communism. He was very critical of his predecessor, Dwight Eisenhower, for allowing a Communist regime to come to power in Cuba.

While Kennedy was in office, he increased both the nation's stores of nuclear weapons and the number of troops that used conventional (non-nuclear) weapons. Even though he did not live to see the day when the United States boosted the number of ground troops in Vietnam and began a sustained bombing campaign there, he had paved the way for this development. During his brief administration, the United States greatly increased support for the anti-Communist South Vietnamese, and by November of 1963, there were sixteen thousand members of the United States military in the country training and advising the South Vietnamese army.

Kennedy was assassinated on November 22, 1963. We will never know how he would have handled the Vietnam war, or the many other proxy wars around the world, had he lived. But he made it clear that he was strongly opposed to Communism.

Kim Il-Sung

Kim Il-Sung was one of the few world leaders who remained in power through the entire Cold War. Kim was born in 1912 to a poor peasant family in Korea during the time that nation was occupied by Japan. His family fled Korea for Manchuria in China when Kim was just a child. He joined the Communist youth movement when he was still a teenager, and during the 1930s, he joined the resistance movement to free Korea from Japanese rule. He came to the attention of the Soviet Army and was sent to the Soviet Union where he received military training. When he returned to Korea in 1945 at the age of thirty-three, he was a Major in the Soviet Army that liberated Korea from the Japanese. When the Soviet Army withdrew from Korea, Kim remained and became the first premier of the People's Democratic Republic of Korea, also known as North Korea, and ruled there with an iron fist from the time it was established in 1948 until his death in 1994.

Though Kim was most aligned with the Soviets, having lived and studied there for many years, he was willing to accept any aid offered that would help him reunify his country and solidify his rule—and the help that saved Korea from being taken over by NATO forces came in part from China.

Once the Korean War had ended, with the country still divided, Kim maintained ties with both the USSR and China and remained extremely hostile toward both South Korea and the United States. However, he did not hew closely to either Maoism or Marxist-Leninist ideology, but instead he took his country in an independent direction, though still a form of Communism. He died in 1994 and passed his rule to his son, Kim Jong Il.

Ho Chi Minh

Ho Chi Minh was born in Vietnam while it was under French colonial rule. (Vietnam was then called French Indo-China.) The French were in charge, but there was still an emperor, though he had no real political power. Ho's father worked at the Imperial Court but lost his job because he made comments criticizing the French colonial government. When he was twenty-one, Ho took a job on a French ship and travelled to Europe, where he lived in Paris and in London. He was one of the founding members of the French Communist Party, and he went to Moscow for training in how to promote worldwide Communism. When he returned to Asia, he founded the Indo-Asian Communist Party. He returned to Vietnam after the Japanese invasion, and he began a Communist movement to gain independence from Japan. When the Japanese were ousted at the end of World War II, the Vietnamese declared their independence, but the French refused to leave. It took eight years for the Vietnamese to force the French to agree to peace talks, and then the country was divided. Ho became president of North Vietnam. Ho continued to fight, determined to unite Vietnam under Communist rule. While Ho was dedicated

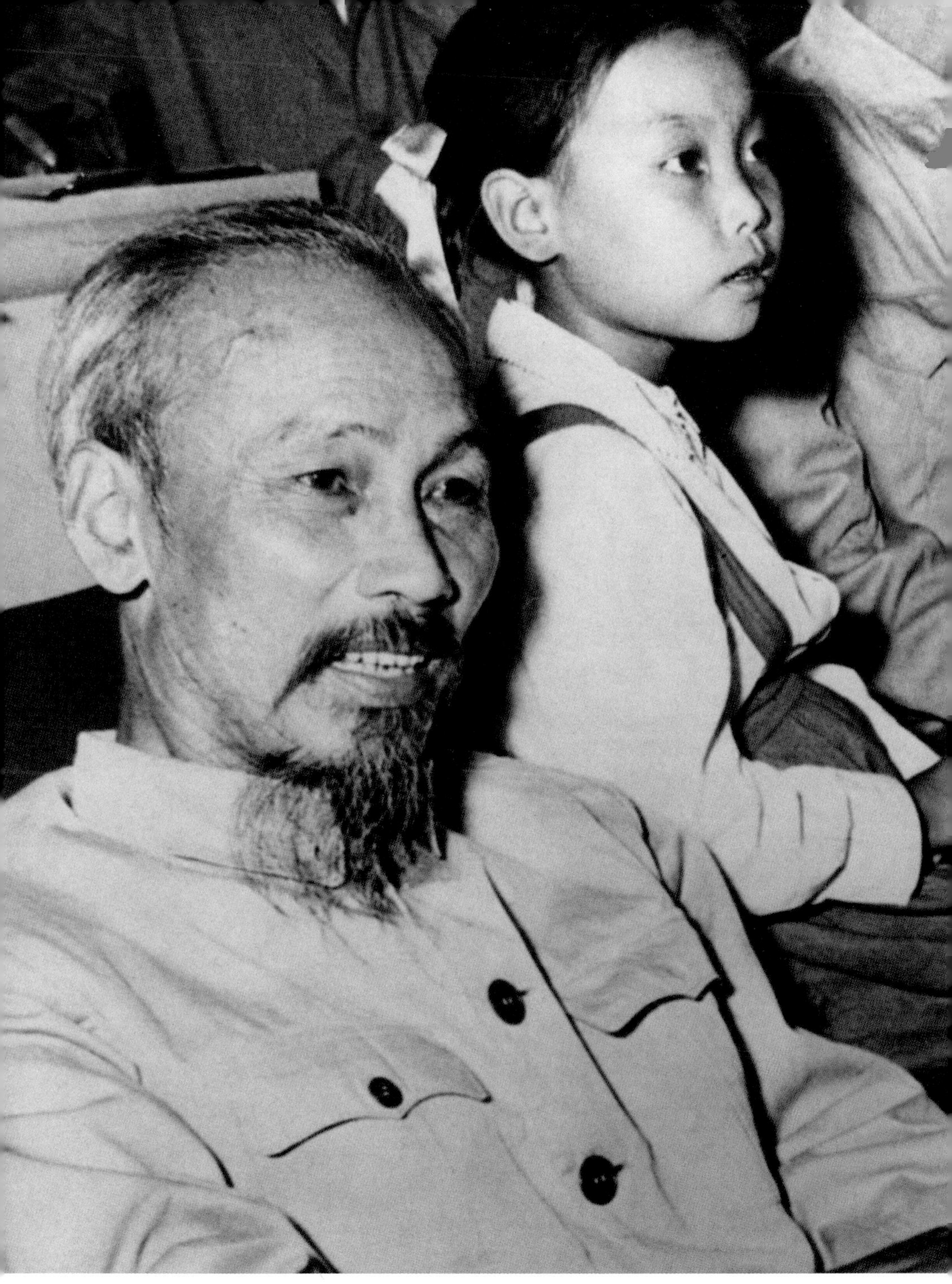

Ho Chi Minh, often called the George Washington of Vietnam, is still remembered with respect and affection in his country.

to the Communist ideal, he was also determined to reunite his country, and because of this he was willing to accept aid from both the USSR and China even though by this time the disagreements between the two countries had become severe.

Ho has been described as the George Washington of Vietnam, and Thomas Jefferson was one of his heroes. The *New York Times* obituary of Ho said of him, "Westerners who knew him were convinced that, whatever his guile in larger political matters, there was no pose in his expressions of feeling for the common people." He was determined to make life better for the Vietnamese people, and he often expressed surprise that the United States, a former colony that had fought for its own independence, should be opposed to another country's fight for independence. He modeled the Vietnamese Declaration of Independence on that of the United States.

He died in 1969, and he did not live to see his country at last united. Saigon, the largest city in the reunited Vietnam, was renamed Ho Chi Minh City in his honor.

Leonid Brezhnev

In 1964, Nikita Khrushchev was replaced as leader of the Soviet Union by Leonid Brezhnev. Brezhnev had come up in the ranks of the Communist Party, and Khrushchev had helped advance his career. Brezhnev was a supporter of Khrushchev until the last few months of Khrushchev's tenure, when Brezhnev led the group of people who arranged to replace Khrushchev. For a short period of time, Brezhnev shared power with Aleksey Kosygin, another person who helped replace Khrushchev, but very soon Brezhnev consolidated power and became the sole head of the Soviet government.

As Soviet leader, Brezhnev developed the Brezhnev Doctrine. In some ways mirroring the Truman Doctrine many years earlier, it outlined the Soviet position regarding foreign policy. The Brezhnev doctrine stated that the USSR had the right to intervene in any nation where the interests of any other Communist country were threatened. Despite

Richard Nixon and Leonid Brezhnev shake hands after signing a historic arms reduction treaty.

the fact that this policy suggested a wide scope for the Soviet Union in international affairs, and Moscow did use it as justification for invading Czechoslovakia in 1968, Brezhnev actually made quite an effort to ease relations with the West and especially the United States during the 1970s.

Nevertheless, Brezhnev supported Soviet allies in proxy wars in Vietnam and in Latin America, and he sent troops to Afghanistan in 1979. He also oversaw a huge build-up of the Soviet military, increasing the store of nuclear weapons as well as conventional forces. In the end, this extreme emphasis on military spending at the expense of the rest of the society severely damaged the Soviet economy. Brezhnev died suddenly in 1982 and made way for a new generation of reformers.

Lyndon B. Johnson

When Kennedy was assassinated in 1963, his vice president, Lyndon Johnson became president. In addition to being in charge of a grief-stricken nation, Johnson found himself managing the nation's role in the civil war in Vietnam, a situation the United States was already deeply involved in.

Unlike Kennedy, Johnson had been very poor growing up, and he had a deep and genuine concern for the underprivileged. As president, he vowed to "end poverty and racial injustice." He pushed through sweeping civil rights legislation and a suite of social legislation called the Great Society, which included guaranteed healthcare for the elderly (Medicare), environmental protection laws, and many programs designed to help lift people out of poverty.

Ironically, much of Johnson's domestic agenda was not unlike what Ho Chi Minh, the leader of North Vietnam, wanted for his people.

After completing Kennedy's term, Johnson was re-elected in a landslide in 1964. But his handling of the Vietnam War was his downfall. In 1965, he sent one hundred thousand ground troops to Vietnam; by 1967, he had sent five hundred thousand. As Johnson committed more and more troops to southeast Asia, the death toll continued to rise, and the American public became increasingly opposed to the war. Johnson responded to the antiwar movement by sending even more soldiers, weapons, and money in an attempt to bring the war to a quick end. Instead, he just became more embroiled in an unwinnable war. The public increasingly blamed Johnson for the war, and his approval ratings plummeted. During the 1940s and 1950s, the call to resist a Communist takeover of the world had been enough of a rallying cry to garner public support for proxy wars with the Soviet Union. By the 1960s, few Americans were concerned about the Communist threat and could not see any strategic benefit to sending Americans to be killed overseas just to keep one more country from having a Communist government. In March of 1968, Johnson announced that he would not seek re-election; his presidency was itself a casualty of the Vietnam War.

Mikhail Gorbachev

Mikhail Gorbachev was the last of the Cold War leaders in the Soviet Union. Several members of Gorbachev's family were victims of Stalin's iron rule and served time in prison

Student protestors at Kent State try to help their fellow student after he was shot by the National Guard.

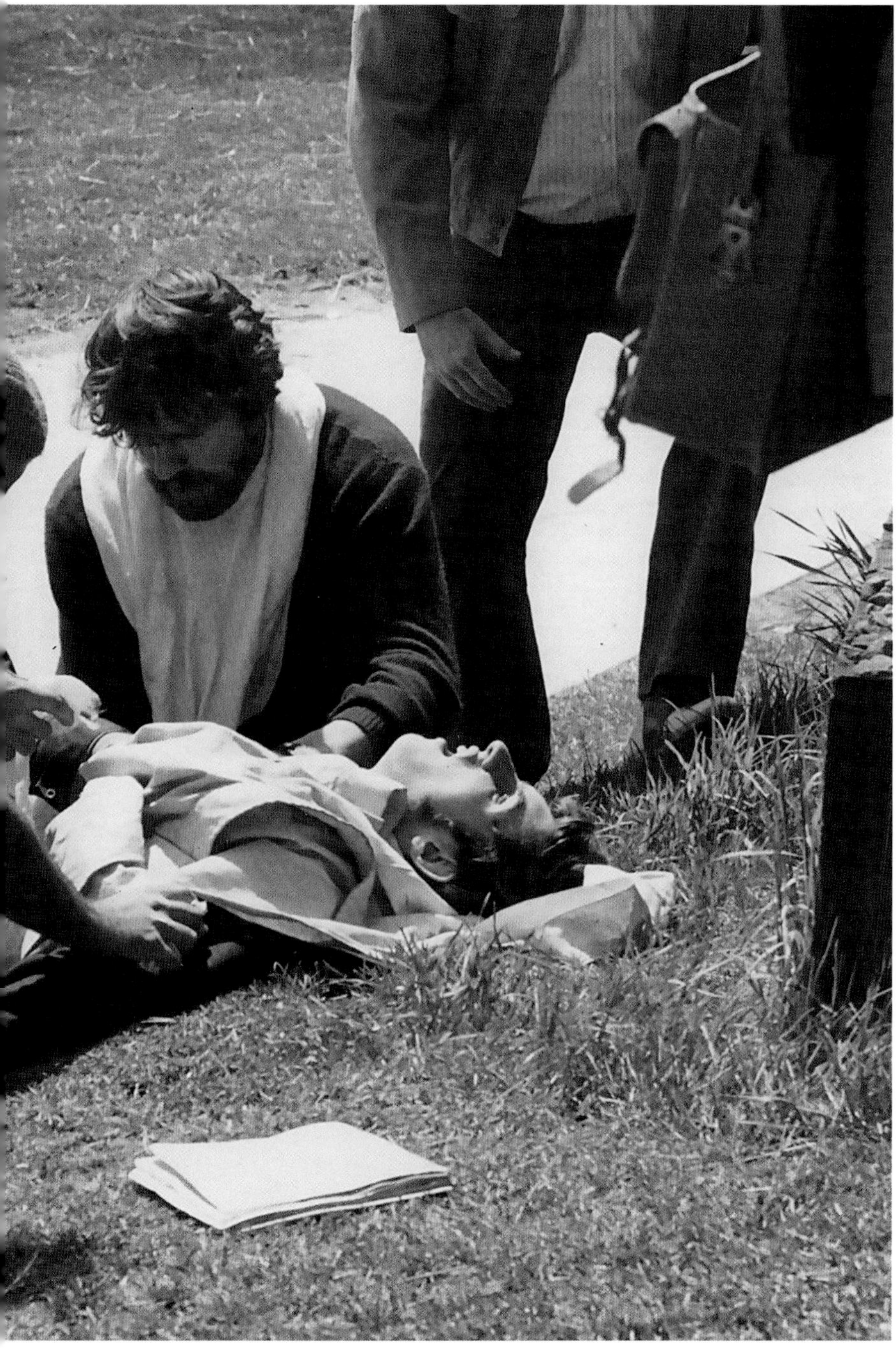

No More War

Early in the Vietnam War, most Americans still believed in the general idea of containment and feared that if the United States did not intervene in Vietnam, more and more countries would fall to Communism. But as the war wore on and casualties (both of American soldiers and Vietnamese civilians) increased, public sentiment shifted. An increase in the number of young men being drafted added to the nation's dissatisfaction with the war. A rapidly growing peace movement saw the war in Vietnam as an unnecessary, even immoral, intrusion into the attempts of a foreign nation to choose its own leaders and government. Those who were less concerned about democracy abroad were swayed by the fact that the war was costing much more than the country could afford.

The antiwar movement was driven by students, who staged protests and occupied administration buildings on college campuses, and during the last years of President Johnson's administration could be heard chanting, "Hey, hey, LBJ, how many kids did you kill today?" The protests only increased after Richard Nixon became president in 1968 and continued to send troops to Vietnam. Most of the protests were peaceful, but occasionally they turned violent. On May 4, 1970, there was a large protest rally at Kent State University in Ohio. The National Guard was called in to break up the rally, and soldiers opened fire on the demonstrators, killing four and wounding nine students. The shootings increased the nation's sympathy for the protest movement, which only increased over the next few years, until the Paris Peace Accords (PPA) were signed in 1973, ending the war in Vietnam.

or in labor camps for various offenses against Stalin's regime. Of course, they were not the only ones. Stalin had killed so many people ("purged" was the word used at the time for eliminating political enemies or people deemed to be enemies of Communism) that there was a gap in leadership between the old guard and younger leaders who had a somewhat different vision for the country. By the time Brezhnev died, a new generation of leadership was ready.

Gorbachev was intelligent and ambitious and rose quickly to the top of the Communist Party in the Soviet Union. However, having grown up during the worst ideological extremes of the Stalin years, and having lived through the economic troubles of the Brezhnev years, he also recognized the need for reforms, and he worked hard to implement them, through more democracy, freedom of speech, and access to information for Soviet citizens. He said, "It was high time to put an end to the rulers' wild cravings and to their highhandedness." He also fostered an increased openness with the West. Gorbachev made agreements with President Ronald Reagan to reduce the numbers of intermediate-range nuclear missiles. During the time that Gorbachev was leader of his country's Communist Party and of the nation, the relationship between the United States and the USSR changed completely. The two superpowers began to cooperate more and see each other less as enemies. Gorbachev removed the remaining Soviet troops from Afghanistan in 1989, ending the last proxy war between the two superpowers. His policies led to the end of the Soviet Union. Gorbachev stepped down as president in 1991.

During the Cuban missile crisis, John Kennedy and Nikita Khrushchev engaged in what were likely the most delicate negotiations of the Cold War.

CHAPTER FOUR

Negotiation and Innovation

As the Cold War wore on, leaders in both the United States and the Soviet Union began to see the world situation as more complex than a simple formula of a planet divided between the free world and the forces of Communism. While the rhetoric continued on both sides, behind the scenes, world leaders were doing a lot more talking, though that wasn't always obvious to the public.

Though there had been a great deal of tough talk between United States President Kennedy and Soviet Premier Khrushchev (Khrushchev at one time said to the United States, "We will bury you"), both men wanted peaceful coexistence between their nations. Unfortunately, Khrushchev's policies were not so popular with the powerful conservative faction of his government back home. His willingness to make deals with the West helped his enemies, who accused him of being soft on the West. They forced him out of office in 1964 to be replaced, after a little political jockeying, by hardliner Leonid Brezhnev.

Though Brezhnev was very much committed to Communist ideology, he also realized that the world had changed. Nations in the Middle East and in Central America were becoming more important, and relations between China and the Soviet Union were becoming more and more strained—at times, the two seemed on the verge of war. And Brezhnev had his own problems at home. While his wing of the party had easily wrested power from Khrushchev, the continued military build-up (much of it for defense of the border with China) was damaging the economy and creating protests and dissent among the people of the USSR and some less hardline party members.

Meanwhile, United States leaders were facing similar problems. In 1968, Richard Nixon was elected president of the United States. Nixon had been elected to Congress on the wave of anti-Communist fervor that led to the Red Scare, and in fact he had served on the House Un-American Activities Committee (HUAC). But now that he was president, he realized that the public was no longer supporting the war in Vietnam, and the military expense was causing economic problems in the United States as well. President Nixon and Secretary of State Henry Kissinger were ready to deal with the Soviets. For the first time, the two nations began to talk seriously about reducing their stores of weapons. This softening of relations between the two countries was known as détente.

SALT

By this time, each country's nuclear arsenal was beyond redundant. They had enough nuclear weapons to destroy each other—and the rest of the world in the bargain—many times over. In 1969, shortly after Nixon took office, the two superpowers began Strategic Arms Limitation Talks (SALT), which would allow each country to stop building nuclear weapons so that they could refocus their resources on their economies. Moscow was motivated to improve relations with the United States for another reason as well. The Soviet agricultural industry had been unable to produce enough food and wanted to be able to buy grain from the United States.

President Richard Nixon and Secretary of State Henry Kissinger at first expanded the Vietnam War and then worked to bring it to a close.

At the same time, Nixon quietly engaged in negotiations to normalize relations with China. Though he met with some resistance from conservative members of his own party, Nixon's deal with China proved to be one of the greatest accomplishments of his presidency. Nixon hoped that warmer relations with both the USSR and China would allow the United States to use its influence with the two countries to play them against each other and weaken their support for North Vietnam. This aspect of the plan did not work. North Vietnamese leader Ho Chi Minh proved brilliant at getting support from both the USSR and China, despite their differences. Nevertheless, these negotiations were the beginning of a long process of easing tensions between the superpowers.

Normalizing relations with China was one of the biggest accomplishments of Nixon's presidency.

The SALT treaty limited production of nuclear weapons, but it did not restrict the deployment of nuclear missiles. Nixon resigned from office in 1972 due to Watergate, a political scandal, but succeeding administrations continued arms limitations negotiations. United States president Jimmy Carter, who was elected in 1976, worked to negotiate SALT II, a new treaty between the United States and the Soviet Union that imposed even further restrictions on the production of missiles and included limits on where they could be based. SALT II was signed in June of 1979. However, it never took effect. When the Soviet Union invaded Afghanistan in December of that year, the United States Senate refused to ratify the treaty.

Two Steps Back, One Huge Step Forward

In the next few years, it seemed as if the improving relations between the Soviet Union and the United States were over. United States president Ronald Reagan, elected in 1980, famously described the Soviet Union as the "evil empire." The superpowers were involved in proxy wars in Asia, Africa, and Central America, and both used these as excuses to continue building their stockpiles of weapons. Reagan stoked anti-Communist fears at home and presented a threatening face to the Soviets by proposing a Strategic Defense Initiative (SDI) that would use space-based lasers to protect the United States from Soviet missiles. Experts said the plan was unworkable, and critics dubbed it "Star Wars." The Soviets, who were falling behind in the arms race as their economic problems worsened, were angry that the United States was still talking about enormous weapons programs, even if defensive ones.

Then in 1982, Brezhnev died suddenly. He was succeeded by Yuri Andropov, who died only fifteen months later, and *his* successor, Konstantin Chernenko, died thirteen months after he took office. These were among the last of the old-style Soviet leaders. Stalin's purges had killed off so many of their generation that the leadership of the country fell to a younger generation with much different views about Communism and the role of the USSR in the world. When Mikhail Gorbachev, then fifty-four years old, became leader of the Soviet Union, he inherited a stagnant economy and a population weary of food shortages and long lines for basic goods. In addition, Moscow could no longer afford to send economic aid to Eastern Bloc countries, and these nations were becoming rebellious. Gorbachev turned his attention from competition with the United States to addressing problems at home. He made many changes in the Soviet system, including economic reforms (**perestroika**, or "restructuring") and increased openness in the government and society at large (**glasnost**, or "openness"). This gave him the political clout he needed to return to the negotiating table with the United States. Reagan, at first resistant, came around quickly, and in 1987, the superpowers agreed to the Intermediate-Range Nuclear Forces (INF) Treaty, an agreement that required them to eliminate their ground-launched ballistic and cruise missiles with a range of five hundred to five thousand kilometers (311 to 3,107 miles) as well as the destruction of the launchers and associated support structures.

Star Wars

Though President Reagan's Strategic Defense Initiative (SDI) was mocked for being more science fiction than science, some missile defense silos were built. A missile defense silo, or launch facility, is an underground structure that can store and launch intercontinental ballistic missiles (ICBMs). While a few tests were conducted, Reagan's plan was dropped after the end of the Cold War and the collapse of the Soviet Union. But the idea didn't really die. There have been several sequels to Reagan's Star Wars idea. During President Bill Clinton's administration in the 1990s, the program was scaled down and renamed the Ballistic Missile Defense Organization (BMDO), but the idea of developing some kind of defense system to protect against intercontinental ballistic missiles was still very much alive.

After the United States was attacked by terrorists (using airplanes, not ballistic missiles) in 2001, the George W. Bush administration dusted off the program, created a new agency, the Missile Defense Agency (MDA), and allocated billions of dollars for maintaining the aging missile silos first built for the program—despite the fact that experts still don't know how to make the plan work. Experts estimate that the United States has spent in the neighborhood of one hundred billion dollars on an idea that would be great if it worked, but so far hasn't come close.

While the superpowers still had competing interests around the world, these treaties reflect the softening of their approaches and definite commitment to working together to lessen the chances of the Cold War turning hot and to reducing the world's store of nuclear weapons. The worst of the proxy wars—Vietnam, for example—ended because neither superpower could afford to keep fighting, and both politicians and the public ceased to be engaged by the rhetoric that had sustained these wars.

Not Just Nukes

Ironically, the technology that kept the Cold War from getting hot was the most destructive weapon ever designed, the atomic bomb. While both nations spent some effort on defense in case of an attack, through building bomb shelters and designing civil defense plans, both operated on the theory of nuclear deterrence: the only way to prevent the other side from using their nuclear weapons was to have more nuclear weapons than they did. Obviously, the logic of this gets muddled when both nations have far more nuclear power than would be needed to destroy the other, but the idea, aptly known as **MAD (mutually assured destruction)**, was the weirdly logical concept that kept forty-five years of proxy wars around the world from turning into a nuclear war between the two superpowers. It also left the world dangerously stocked with nuclear weapons. But the technological innovations of weaponry and its delivery systems didn't stop with a weapon that everyone wanted and no one wanted to use.

A B-52 bomber drops its payload.

Flying Fortresses

The planes that dropped atomic bombs on two Japanese cities, Hiroshima and Nagasaki, were B-29 bombers. They were state-of-the-art at the time, but they had some limitations in the Cold War. They had a range of only 4,200 miles (6,759 kilometers) and were vulnerable to fighter jets. The United States began working on a series of upgraded bombers, culminating in the B-52 Stratofortress, which could carry a 70,000-pound (31,751.5 kilogram) bomb load, and with the development of refueling planes, could be refueled in the air, giving it a virtually unlimited range. Though designed to carry a nuclear payload, B-52s were used extensively in Vietnam for delivering conventional bombs. Meanwhile, the Soviets built the Myasishchev M-4 Bison, a long-range bomber similar to the B-52. Rumors that the Soviets had

The Birth of the Internet

Not all of the technology that was developed in response to the Cold War was weapons technology. After the Soviets launched Sputnik, and the possibility of a nuclear strike on American soil was suddenly greater, the US Department of Defense was keen to find a way to disseminate information in the event of a nuclear attack. It was important that the means of communication as well as the computers that operated the weapons were not all in a single location that could be taken out with one bomb.

In 1969, the Advanced Research Projects Agency (ARPA), a part of the military, developed a computer network called ARPANET (Advanced Research Projects Agency Network) that linked widely scattered academic

The internet that we take for granted today was developed during the Cold War as a way to facilitate and decentralize communications among defense contractors.

and research organizations working with the defense department. Now they could share information across the country. Other, similar networks were soon formed, but there was no standard communications format for these networks to talk to each other. In 1983, a new communications protocol, called Transfer Control Protocol/Internetwork Protocol (TCP/IP) was developed, allowing different kinds of computer networks to share a universal language. This was the beginning of the Internet.

The decentralization of information served another purpose as well, one the people who designed it were aware of (even if the **Pentagon** didn't give it much thought). A decentralized source of information and communication makes it hard for governments and corporations to control information and access to it. It was a clever way to hold the United States government to its promise of freedom and to give citizens of totalitarian governments contact with the rest of the world.

far more Bisons than they actually had led the United States to build even more B-52s. The arms race was not just about nukes, but about their delivery systems as well.

Game Changer

By 1957, both superpowers had medium-range rockets that could deliver nuclear bombs. The Soviet Union was in range of US rockets placed in Europe, but the Soviets had none that could reach the United States. Then in 1957, the Soviets launched *Sputnik*, a satellite about the size of a basketball, into Earth's orbit, demonstrating that it had a rocket capable of delivering missiles all the way to the United States. Both countries had been working on Intercontinental Ballistic Missiles (ICBMs), but the USSR got there first. ICBMs are more dangerous than bombers because they move at such high speeds that they are virtually impossible to shoot down. Once the Soviets had demonstrated their missiles, the United States upped its program, and by the end of 1959, the United States had six armed ICBMs. In the next three years, that number increased to 203. ICBMs added another element to the arms race even though these weapons were a lot more expensive to build than just the nuclear bombs. The most dangerous of the United States's ICBMs was the Minuteman missile and the Peacekeeper. The Peacekeeper could fly more than six thousand miles (9,656.1 km) and could deliver ten nuclear warheads each targeted to a different location. The Soviets had their own multi-target ICBM, the RM-36M, but in the United States, it was known as the SS-Satan.

The Space Race

The launch of *Sputnik* was the first indication that the USSR had ICBM technology. But it was more than that. The conflict between the United States and the Soviet Union was as much a propaganda war as anything else. Leaders of both nations used propaganda to gain support at home and to intimidate their opponents. When the Soviets launched *Sputnik*, Khrushchev lost no time in extolling the technological superiority of his nation. Both countries had a space program, and the USSR had just shown that its program was more advanced. The United States responded by creating the National Aeronautics and Space Administration (NASA) and passing the National Defense Education Act (NDEA), which poured funds into science education and reformed school curriculum to better emphasize mathematics and science. Attempts by the United States to launch its own satellite weren't as successful—at least not right away. It was several months and several embarrassing failures later before the United States got its own satellite in orbit. A space race ensued in which each nation tried to reach the next goal of space exploration ahead of the other and to prove that its form of government was best suited to making great technological innovations. The space race was largely symbolic, but at the same time, developing the technology to get into space went hand in hand with the technology to wage war.

Ronald Reagan, who once called the USSR "the evil empire," and Soviet leader Mikhail Gorbachev meet for the first time, in Geneva in 1985.

CHAPTER FIVE

The Legacy of Superpower Rivalries and Proxy Warfare

The Cold War began with a bang, or perhaps a series of bangs—the dramatic end of World War II, the blockade of Berlin, Stalin's creation of what Winston Churchill dubbed the Iron Curtain. But it ended with a whimper. The Berlin Wall fell; the Iron Curtain was dropped; the Soviet Union disassembled. During the middle 1980s, relations between the United States and the Soviet Union improved, and by the mid-1990s, Soviet republics declared independence.

How did United States and Soviet relations improve? The ideological differences that underpinned much of the conflict between the superpowers became diluted over the years, as economic conditions in the Soviet Union created a greater desire for trade with the West and freer economies at home. Social conditions in the United States gave birth to a stronger sense of equality and a more equal distribution of wealth. While the United States certainly did not become a Communist country, and the Soviet Union never embraced capitalism, Lyndon Johnson's Great Society reforms and Gorbachev's implementation of perestroika and glasnost diluted the contrasts between the two nations and took the bite out of the rhetoric.

By the end of the Cold War, citizens of both nations began to see the other superpower as a complex society, rather than an "evil empire." Recall that when President Reagan called the USSR the "evil empire" in his address to the National Association of Evangelicals in Orlando, Florida, he defended a Judeo-Christian worldview in contrast to the Soviet Union's totalitarianism. He maintained that this was the fundamental distinction at the core of the battle between the two nations: "While America's military strength is important, let me add here that I've always maintained that the struggle now going on for the world will never be decided by bombs or rockets, by armies or military might. The real crisis we face today is a spiritual one; at root, it is a test of moral will and faith." Now the few proxy wars that were still being fought by the end of the Cold War were less about belief systems than about oil. Economics had trumped beliefs and ideology.

Walls Start Falling

By the late 1980s, the Soviet Union was relaxing its grasp on the nations it had invaded after World War II. Perhaps the most poignant symbol of a rapidly changing world occurred on November 9, 1989. The Soviet-allied East German government announced that it would grant visas to anyone who wanted to visit the West. That night, a crowd gathered at the Berlin Wall demanding to be let out. The guards opened the gates, and people poured through to freedom. East Germans began to celebrate in the streets—families who had been separated for almost thirty years could now be reunited—and then the crowd began to tear down the Berlin Wall.

Meanwhile, in Eastern Europe, walls were coming down as well. During the height of the Cold War, any attempts by Eastern Bloc nations to resist Soviet authority were mercilessly crushed. In 1954, one thousand Soviet tanks rolled into Hungary to quash a rebellion there. In 1968, when the leader of the Communist Party in Czechoslovakia began to make reforms (including less central control of the economy and a greater voice for non-Communist parties), and the public supported him with protests against the Soviet's position, the Soviet army moved into that country to brutally crush this attempt to challenge Soviet authority. These actions damaged relations between the superpowers, but never led to proxy wars because the United States saw this as the USSR defending established territory rather than expanding its scope.

But by the late 1980s, the desire for the reforms like the ones being made in the Soviet Union under the leadership of Mikhail Gorbachev spread to Eastern Europe. The USSR also no longer had the money to enforce its will on these nations. They quickly declared their independence from Soviet regimes, and Moscow did not interfere. After negotiating with President Reagan for reductions in the number of nuclear weapons of each country, Gorbachev drastically reduced the size of the Soviet Army and removed

People around the world celebrated when the Berlin Wall was destroyed.

troops from Eastern Europe. In 1989, Gorbachev met with newly-elected United States president George H. W. Bush and said, "We don't consider you an enemy anymore." The Cold War was coming to an end.

The End of Proxy Wars

The end of the Cold War left Latin America with more democracy, though not necessarily with less violence and corruption. But it did remove at least one excuse for division. Communism versus capitalism, with the superpowers each supporting a side, was no longer the defining framework. In 1992, Mexican novelist Carlos Fuentes told the *New York Times*, "The fact that we can see the problems in their proper perspective rather than through a mask of anti-Communism or pro-Communism is the beginning of the resolution of those problems on their real terms."

In Africa, some Communist groups still survived, but without financial support from Moscow, most died out, though civil wars continued in many places on the African continent. By the end of the Cold War, many countries in the Middle East were very unstable. Even now, both the United States and Russia are still deeply involved in Syria, and they have differing ideas about who should rule there. Some experts have said that this is a new proxy war between the United States and Russia. The last proxy war between the Cold War superpowers, however, ended in 1989 when Gorbachev pulled the remaining Soviet troops from Afghanistan.

The Exercise That Almost Got Real

The Cuban missile crisis was not the only close call during the Cold War. In 1983, the United States and its NATO allies conducted a yearly war games exercise—and it was just an exercise—called Able Archer. It involved four thousand NATO troops moving across Western Europe in response to a simulated Soviet invasion of Yugoslavia that had turned nuclear. For the 1983 exercise, they added a few embellishments, such as planes rolling out of hangars carrying very realistic-looking dummy missiles.

This was not long after the Soviets had recently shot down a Korean airplane that had strayed into Soviet airspace because they thought it was an American spy plane. Relations between the superpowers were already tense when the exercise took place. The Soviets thought that the exercise was a cover for an actual nuclear assault on their territory. What better way to get the jump on them than by disguising an attack as a war game? They responded by arming a dozen aircraft with nuclear missiles. NATO thought this was the USSR's own war games. Meanwhile, the Soviets were no doubt somewhat frantically trying to decide how long to wait before launching a nuclear response. Fortunately, they figured out what was going on in the nick of time, and the world was once again saved from nuclear devastation.

It's possible that this extremely close call gave Soviet leaders—among them Mikhail Gorbachev—a huge motivation to bring the Cold War to a peaceful end.

By fighting their conflicts with each other by proxy and never coming in direct conflict on either nation's soil, the United States and the Soviet Union miraculously avoided stumbling into nuclear war. However, the Cold War remained "cold" only from the perspective of nuclear war and direct confrontation between the superpowers. For the millions of American and Soviet soldiers and even more millions of civilians who died in these many proxy wars, the Cold War was very hot indeed.

The End of an Empire

As the Cold War ended, so did one of the superpowers. In 1989, Gorbachev began the process of restructuring the government of the Soviet Union, creating the office of a presidency and allowing for multi-party elections. This democratization of the USSR left Gorbachev caught between a pluralist movement, headed by Boris Yeltsin, that wanted more and faster democratic and economic reforms, and hardliners in his own Communist Party who were solidly against his reforms. In addition to these troubles, several of the nations that made up the Soviet Union, inspired by Moscow's loosening of its control over Eastern European countries, began to demand independence. The USSR responded to democratic uprisings in Latvia and Lithuania by sending in tanks. Then in 1991, hardliners in the Communist Party staged a coup against Gorbachev, sending troops to hold him and his family under house arrest at their country home. They weren't as effective at containing Yeltsin, however, and he took advantage of having Gorbachev temporarily

Boris Yeltsin addresses the public during the 1991 coup that overthrew the USSR's Communist government.

out of the way to rally popular support and seize power. Yeltsin dissolved the Central Committee of the Communist Party, banned party activities, and installed a democratic government. A few days later, two more members of the USSR, Ukraine and Belarus, declared their independence. Gorbachev, released from house arrest, returned to Moscow and resigned. The Soviet Union quietly disintegrated. On December 25, 1991, the Soviet hammer-and-sickle flag was lowered from the Kremlin, and the Russian flag was raised. The Communist Party is still active in Russia, though it is not in power, and in any case, is more like the Social Democratic parties of Western Europe than the old-style Communist Party of the Cold War years.

By 2016, there were only five Communist countries remaining in the world: China, Vietnam, North Korea, Laos, and Cuba. China, though still run by a Communist government, has a capitalist economy. In 2016, the United States restored diplomatic relations with Cuba, the lone Communist country in the Western hemisphere.

The Lasting Impact of the Cold War

During the Cold War, the stakes were high and the goals and strategies of the proxy wars were complex, but the worldview was simple: The United States represented capitalism on one side, and the Soviet Union represented Communism on the other side. After the Cold War, things became anything but simple.

After forty-five years of proxy wars around the world, the United States public had become accustomed to its government intervening in the affairs of other countries and playing the role of policeman of the world. In the post–Cold War years, Washington found itself involved in more conflicts in other nations, sometimes for humanitarian reasons and sometimes to protect important resources, such as oil. Prior to World War I, the United States had favored a policy of isolationism—it preferred to tend to its own affairs and let the rest of the world tend to theirs. Entry into World War I was something of an exception to this policy, but events at the end of World War II showed that intervention

The Russian flag flies once again over the Kremlin.

in the rest of the world was now the norm rather than the exception. The end of the Cold War showed that the policy was permanent. The genie of interventionism could not be put back in the bottle.

However, if government policies had changed, so had public opinion—and so had the power of public opinion. Despite widespread support for military interventions, such as the ouster of Iraq from Kuwait in 1990, the end of the Cold War left citizens in both Russia and the United States wary of getting involved in proxy wars, and their governments more aware of the power of their citizens to influence foreign policy. Dissent over the worsening economy in the Soviet Union gave Gorbachev little choice other than reform. The war protest movement in the United States was a major factor in forcing that country to find a way out of the hopeless war in Vietnam. After Vietnam, the United States population was far more aware of and vocal about its opposition to the government's activities in Latin America and Africa. And after Gorbachev's reforms, the population of the Soviet Union was far more aware of what its government was up to.

The proxy wars of the Cold War could be likened to two superpowers playing an ideological chess game with other countries as the pawns. By the end of the era, the concerns of people on the ground in the countries where these wars were being fought, the people whose lives and futures were in the balance, were being taken into account far more than they had been before. After the Cold War, people were much less willing to sit by and watch their governments wage real wars with real deaths over abstract concepts—and sometimes even very concrete resources, such as oil. Both the United States and Russia are very much involved in conflicts in the Middle East, but no longer are they trying to simplify the issues.

But if ideology is no longer the driving force behind the affairs of the United States and Russia, in other places it very much is. Soon after the end of the Cold War, both the United States and Russia found themselves fighting and supporting fighters even though they were no longer in proxy wars against each other. This time, they were supporting

United States secretary of state John Kerry and Iranian foreign minister Mohammad Javad Sharif shake hands on a historic agreement between their two nations.

highly organized but unlocalized groups of people who were trying to impose the ideology of a kind of Islamic fundamentalism on the oil-rich nations of the Middle East and using terrorism against Western nations and Russia to influence their policies. It remains to be seen how much the United States and Russia learned from the Cold War and whether those lessons will be of any use against a new threat that uses ideology to rally its supporters and goad its enemies.

One thing is certain, though. Ideologies may have changed, but technology has not. Even though the Cold War ended without nuclear war, and the two superpowers shook hands and ended on relatively friendly terms, the world is not necessarily a safer place. Chess is still being played, only more players have the technology that once only the superpowers and a few of their allies had. As of 2016, nine nations had nuclear weapons: Russia, the United States, China, India, Israel, France, North Korea, Pakistan, and the United Kingdom.

In 2012, on the 50th anniversary of the Cuban Missile Crisis, the United States and its allies were working to negotiate a deal with Iran to delay their nuclear program—a situation one expert described as the Cuban Missile Crisis in slow motion. In 2016, North Korea announced that it had completed its fifth test of a nuclear warhead.

Sadly, the world is not safer now that the Cold War has ended, but perhaps after forty-five years of proxy wars and a delicate dance to avoid using the most dangerous weapon ever developed, the world is a little bit smarter.

Chronology

1918 World War I ends.

1945 World War II ends.

1948 The Soviets blockade West Berlin.

1949 The Soviet Union develops nuclear weapons. NATO is founded.

1950 The Korean War begins.

1951 President Truman relieves General Douglas MacArthur of command.

1953 The Korean War ends.

1954 The Vietnam War begins.

1955 Warsaw Pact is founded.

1957 The Soviet Union launches *Sputnik*.

1961 The Berlin Wall is built. The United States supports revolutionaries' attempt at invasion of Cuba at the Bay of Pigs.

1962 The Cuban Missile Crisis unfolds.

1965 The United States commences a troop build-up in Vietnam.

1970	Four students are killed and nine injured at a war protest at Kent State University.
1972	The SALT treaty is negotiated, beginning détente.
1973	The Paris Peace Accords (PPA) are signed, formally ending United States's involvement in Vietnam.
1975	The Vietnam War ends.
1979	Marxist Sandinistas overthrow the United States-supported regime in Nicaragua; civil war between Marxists and a US-supported government erupts in El Salvador.
1989	The Berlin Wall comes down; Soviet forces leave Afghanistan.
1991	The Soviet Union is dissolved.

Glossary

capitalism An economic and political system in which a nation's wealth is controlled by private owners rather than the state.

collectivization The process of abolishing private property and returning ownership to the people or the state.

Communism An economic and political system in which there is no private ownership and a nation's wealth is controlled by the state.

convene To call a meeting or gather for a meeting.

coup The sudden and often violent overthrow of a government or other power structure.

fascism An extreme right-wing authoritarian, dictatorial form of government.

glasnost A policy introduced by Mikhail Gorbachev that was meant to open up the Soviet government and allow for information to be exchanged more freely.

guerrilla war War conducted primarily by small bands of independent fighters, rather than a large, centrally controlled military.

ideology A system of deeply held ideas and beliefs that inform political or economic policy.

innuendo A suggestion or hint that disparages someone without making a direct accusation.

Kremlin The site of the Soviet (now Russian) government. Often used to refer to the government itself.

mutually assured destruction (MAD) The doctrine of military strategy in which the use of nuclear weapons would cause annihilation of both the attacker and its enemy.

nationalize To bring property, a business, or an industry under government control.

parallel Latitude line.

Pentagon The headquarters of the US Department of Defense, often used to refer to the US military.

perestroika Government policy introduced by Mikhail Gorbachev in the Soviet Union during the 1980s that called for reforming and renewing the Soviet economy.

propaganda Information, typically biased, that is used to promote an idea or viewpoint.

radical An idea or person that supports dramatic social change.

Red Army The Army of the Soviet Union, prior to 1946.

USSR The Union of Soviet Socialist Republics, also known as the Soviet Union, was governed by the Communist Party.

Bibliography

Axelrod, Alan. *The Real History of the Cold War: A New Look at the Past*. New York: Sterling, 2009.

Brand, H. W. *The General vs. The President: MacArthur and Truman at the Brink of Nuclear War*. New York: Doubleday, 2016.

Byrne, Malcolm. "The 1956 Hungarian Revolution: A History in Documents." National Security Archive, November 4, 2002. http://nsarchive.gwu.edu/NSAEBB/NSAEBB76/.

Doward, Jamie. "How a NATO War Game Took the World to Brink of Nuclear Disaster." *The Guardian*, November 2, 2013. http://www.theguardian.com/uk-news/2013/nov/02/nato-war-game-nuclear-disaster.

Dumbbell, John. *President Lyndon Johnson and Soviet Communism*. Manchester, UK: Manchester University Press, 2004.

Gaddis, John Lewis. *The Cold War: A New History*. New York: Penguin, 2005.

Golden, Tim. "After the Cold War: Views form Latin America: Sweeping Political Changes Leave Latin Poor Still Poor." *New York Times*, May 30, 1992.

http://www.nytimes.com/1992/05/30/world/after-cold-war-views-latin-america-sweeping-political-changes-leave-latin-poor.html?pagewanted=all.

Kifner, John. "Four Kent State Students Killed by Troops." *New York Times*, May 4, 1970. http://www.nytimes.com/learning/general/onthisday/big/0504.html.

LaFeber, Walter. *America, Russia, and the Cold War*. New York: McGraw Hill, 2008.

McMahon, Robert J. *The Cold War in the Third World*. New York: Oxford University Press, 2013.

"People and Events: Berlin Blockade." American Experience. Accessed October 20, 2016. https://www.pbs.org/wgbh/amex/bomb/peopleevents/pandeAMEX49.html.

"Sputnik and the Dawn of the Space Age." NASA. October 10, 2007. http://history.nasa.gov/sputnik/.

"Treaty Banning Nuclear Weapons Tests in the Atmosphere, in Outer Space and Under Water." US Department of State. Accessed October 2016. http://www.state.gov/t/isn/4797.htm.

Tucker, Robert C., ed. *The Marx-Engels Reader*. New York: W. W. Norton & Company, 1972.

Further Information

Books

Axelrod, Alan. *The Real History of the Cold War: A New Look at the Past*. New York: Sterling Publishing, 2009.

Beyer, Mark. *Nuclear Weapons and the Cold War*. New York: Rosen Publishing Group, 2005.

Fitzgerald, Brian. *McCarthyism: The Red Scare*. Minneapolis: Compass Point Books, 2007.

Myers, Walter Dean. *Fallen Angels*. New York: Scholastic, 2008.

Websites

BBC History: The Korean War

http://www.bbc.co.uk/history/worldwars/coldwar/korea_hickey_01.shtml

This website gives an overview of the Cold War turning hot during the Korean War.

History Channel: Red Scare

http://www.history.com/topics/cold-war/red-scare

This website from the History Channel explores the House Un-American Activities Committee (HUAC) and its role in the Red Scare.

Miller Center

http://millercenter.org

As an affiliate of the University of Virginia, the Miller Center offers an in-depth reference resource to American presidents as well as various history lessons.

National Archives: The Cold War

https://www.archives.gov/research/foreign-policy/cold-war

The National Archives provides important records that document the Cold War era.

Videos

Escalation of the Vietnam War by Lyndon B. Johnson

http://aptv.pbslearningmedia.org/resource/pres10.socst.ush.now.escalate/escalation-of-the-vietnam-war-by-lbj/

This video allows viewers to see archival photographs and newsreel footage in addition to interviews that document Lyndon Johnson's decision-making process during the Vietnam War.

Truman: The Beginning of the Cold War

http://aptv.pbslearningmedia.org/resource/pres10.socst.ush.now.coldwar/the-beginning-of-the-cold-war/

This video includes interviews and photographs that allow viewers to study Harry Truman's efforts to prevent the spread of Communism after World War II.

Index

Page numbers in **boldface** are illustrations. Entries in **boldface** are glossary terms.

Afghanistan, 50–51, 58, 68, 73, 79
Africa, 50, 61, 96, 102
arms race, 7, 53, 57
atomic bombs, 5, 82

Bay of Pigs, 44, 62
Berlin Wall, 23, 59, 91–93
bombers, 83–88
Brezhnev, Leonid, 66–68, 75–76, 80, 89
Brezhnev Doctrine, 67–68

capitalism, 7
Central America, 43–48, 76
China, 42, 63, 100
Cold War, 8, 28, 35, 48, 56, 58, 63, 75, 91–98
collectivization, 57
Communism, 7, 29, 31, 33, 34, 56, 57, 59, 61, 62–63, 64, 80, 96
convened, 37
coup, 6
Cuba, 43–44, 46, 48, 59, 62
Cuban Missile Crisis, 59, 61, 62, 97, 104

East Germany (German Democratic Republic), 25

fascism, 11
free-enterprise capitalism, 29, 31

glasnost, 80, 92
Gorbachev, Mikhail, 51, 69–73, 80, **90**, 93, 96, 97, 98–99, 102
Greece, civil war in, 32–33
guerrilla war, 41

ideology, 11
innuendo, 36
internet, 84–85
interventionism, 100–102
Iron Curtain, 16–20, 91

Johnson, Lyndon B., 68–69, 92

Kennedy, John F., 44, 46, 61–63, **74**, 75
Khrushchev, Nikita, 59–61, 66, **74**, 75
Kim Il-Sung, 63–64
Korea, 33–40
Korean War, 35, 54, 63
Kremlin, 38, 99

Latin America, 61, 68, 96, 102

MacArthur, General Douglas, 38–40, 53–55
MAD, 82
Marx, Karl, 12–13
McCarthy, Joseph, 36–37
Middle East, 48, 76, 96, 102–104
Minh, Ho Chi, 40, 64–66
mutually assured destruction (MD), 82

National Defense Education Act (NDEA), 89
nationalized, 44
National Security Act, 22
NATO (North Atlantic Treaty Organization), 58, 63, 97
Nixon, Richard, 76, 79
North Atlantic Treaty Organization (NATO), 22
North Korea, 63
nuclear weapons, arsenal of, 25, 44, 76

parallel, 33, 38, 40, 55
Pentagon, 85
perestroika, 80, 92
propaganda, 7
proxy wars, 9, 28–29, 40, 43, 46, 50–51, 53, 58, 68, 73, 79, 96–98, 100, 102

radical, 12
Reagan, Ronald, 73, 79, **90**, 93
Red Army, 57
Red Scare, the, 36, 76

SALT, 76–79
South Korea, 64
Sputnik, 88, 89
Stalin, Joseph, 14–15, 20, **52**, 56, 57–59
star wars, 79–81
Strategic Arms Limitation Talks (SALT), 76–79

Truman, Harry, 15, **52**, 55, 55–56
Truman Doctrine, 21, 33, 35, 56, 67

USSR, 11, 14, 15, 21, 29, 99

Vietnam War, 40–43, 62–63, 69, 76, 82, 102

World War II, 5, 6, 20

Yeltsin, Boris, 98–99

About the Author

Avery Elizabeth Hurt grew up in a city with a naval base, where she would sit in school and devise plans for sneaking back home when a nuclear war between the Soviet Union and the United States began—an event she then believed was inevitable. Fortunately she was wrong, but the experience did lead to a lifelong interest in Soviet policy and US-Soviet relations. In college, she minored in political science and took several courses in Soviet and East German history and politics. She is the author of many books for children and young adults, most of them about things much less stressful than the Cold War. She keeps a chunk of the Berlin Wall on her desk.